Dave has a raft.
Dave sets sail on his raft.

MW00814103

1

2

Dave sails on the lake.
It is fun to sail on a raft.
Dave waves to Big Ben.

It rains on Dave.
And it hails on Dave.
The big waves toss the raft.

3

4

The raft tips.
The sail rips.
But Big Ben has fun.

The big waves toss the raft.
The big waves tip the raft.
And Dave lands in the lake.

5

6 The big waves toss Dave.
Can he make it to the raft?

Dave can not make it to the raft.

Dave nabs Big Ben's tail.
Big Ben is a pal.
He takes Dave to the raft.

7

8

Dave makes it to the raft.
Dave is safe.
He waves to Big Ben.